THE
LASTINGMATTERS™
ORGANIZER

Where loved ones find
what matters most

BARBARA BATES SEDORIC

LastingMatters
P.O. Box 2
New Castle, NH 03854
www.LastingMatters.com
ISBN 978-0692028544

To Tom and Boo, for your unending

support, guidance and love.

To my mother Nonnie, whose life ended

suddenly and without adequate preparation.

I hope we honored your wishes in the end.

Once you have completed

The LastingMatters™ Organizer, you

should distribute it to trusted family

members, your estate attorney or

financial advisor for safekeeping.

You may also consider keeping your

copy in a safe place and letting your

family know where it is.

This book belongs to:

Welcome to The LastingMatters™ Organizer

On a sunny, bright morning in May 2006, my world was turned upside down.

I received a call from my brother that my mother had suddenly died. There was no warning. She was not ill and I had just spoken to her the night before. It was the very last thing I expected to hear. I was incredibly close to my mother and my heart was breaking.

In the depths of this sudden, horrific grief, my dad, my brother, and I were immediately thrown into the mountainous task of making urgent decisions and instant arrangements with no map, no directions, and no clear idea what "Nonnie" would have wanted us to do to honor her remarkable life.

The days following her death were so chaotic that grieving had to take a back seat to what felt like an endless trail of paperwork.

We spent countless hours searching for documents, double-checking facts and details about her life for her obituary, wracking our brains to remember conversations we had years ago, and making and answering a multitude of hurried phone calls. We ran copious errands, fought red tape, and had meetings with attorneys, funeral directors, clergy, florists, doctors and insurance agents. I was overwhelmed, exhausted, emotionally wrung out, and worried about how we would ever finalize the myriad of details, sort through her personal effects, and most of all, finally honor what we only guessed her wishes might have been.

The irony of it all is that Nonnie would have hated that. She would have hated that at the end of her life she became a burden to us. I learned a very hard lesson a very hard way, but Nonnie also ended up giving me a real gift: the gift of preparedness.

Death is inevitable, and everyone dies. Yet it is extraordinarily difficult to face and to discuss with loved ones. So we don't. It's also very difficult to think about all the things we need to do to "get our affairs in order." Where does one even begin? And when?

The answer is here, and now.

The LastingMatters Organizer is designed to help you begin to consider, compile, document and determine how and what you want your loved ones to know upon your death, as well as your end-of-life preferences. Taking time to capture your personal information and intentions will greatly reduce the costs, time, guesswork, potential family conflicts, and stress associated with your death. And keeping all of your information safely located in one place will help your loved ones find far more than just your intentions. It will help them find peace of mind.

It is my sincerest hope that my experience offers your family the gift of preparedness during an emotionally challenging time. What a gift you are giving to those you love and those you will leave behind. Nonnie would have approved wholeheartedly!

Carpe Diem,

Barb

Barb Sedoric

Please share your story with me at www.LastingMatters.com

"By failing to prepare, you are preparing to fail."

-BENJAMIN FRANKLIN

TABLE OF CONTENTS

CHAPTER 1

IMMEDIATE MATTERS

"The single biggest problem in communication is the illusion that it has taken place."

–GEORGE BERNARD SHAW

Instructions for loved ones to help them in the days immediately following your death.

Whether your death is sudden or expected, your loved ones will be dealing with a lot of emotion in the period right after your passing. Unfortunately, this is a time when family and friends will need to make immediate and critical decisions.

This chapter will walk you through the essential information your loved ones need in order to make final arrangements in the days and weeks immediately following your death.

In this chapter

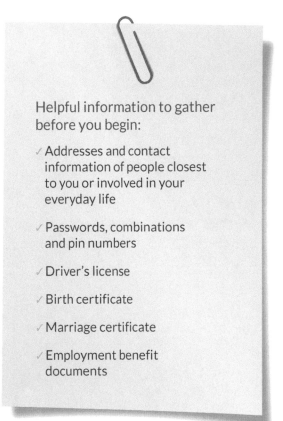

Helpful information to gather before you begin:

✓ Addresses and contact information of people closest to you or involved in your everyday life

✓ Passwords, combinations and pin numbers

✓ Driver's license

✓ Birth certificate

✓ Marriage certificate

✓ Employment benefit documents

1 | A Personal Note

Help your family and friends organize, coordinate and communicate with one another by designating a person (or persons) who you'd like to be in charge of your final arrangements.

To my loved ones:

o Yes
I have filled out this section and would like you to review it.

o No
I have not provided information as this section is not relevant to me.

I want .... to be the point person in my family and to be in charge.

Contact information:

....

....

....

A note to my family:

....

....

....

....

....

....

....

....

2 List of People to Notify

Who would you like to be notified in the event of your death?

To my loved ones:

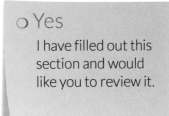

○ Yes
I have filled out this section and would like you to review it.

○ No
I have not provided information as this section is not relevant to me.

I have made a list of people to notify

○ Yes, I have a list   ○ No, I do not have a list

Location of existing list:

If you do not have an existing list, you may list names, phone numbers, email addresses and/or physical addresses of people that you wish to be notified:

3 Power of Attorney

A general power of attorney directive names someone that you trust to act as your agent in financial matters if you are unable to speak for yourself.

To my loved ones:

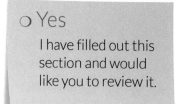

○ Yes
I have filled out this section and would like you to review it.

○ No
I have not provided information as this section is not relevant to me.

Estate attorney

Contact:

....

....

Durable general power of attorney

○ Yes, I have a general power of attorney directive   ○ No, I do not have a general power of attorney directive

Location of document:

....

....

Copies of general power of attorney

○ Yes, I have copies   ○ No, I do not have copies

Location of copies:

....

....

4 | Autopsy

A physician cannot order an autopsy on a patient without the consent of the next of kin, even at academic institutions or hospitals, so documenting your wishes is important. The next of kin also has the right to limit the scope of the autopsy (for example, excluding the brain from evaluation or limiting the procedure to examination of the abdomen) if he/she wishes.

To my loved ones:

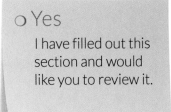

o Yes
I have filled out this section and would like you to review it.

o No
I have not provided information as this section is not relevant to me.

I wish to have an autopsy

○ Yes
○ Yes, with limitations

List of limitations:

....

....

....

○ No
○ No preference (my loved ones may decide on my behalf)

5 | Organ or Body Donation

To my loved ones:

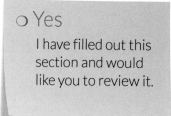

o Yes
I have filled out this section and would like you to review it.

o No
I have not provided information as this section is not relevant to me.

I would like to be an organ or body donor

○ Yes   ○ No   ○ No preference (My loved ones may decide on my behalf)

Donor card

○ Yes, I have a donor card   ○ No, I do not have a donor card

Location of card(s):

Contact information:

I want to donate my body

○ Yes, I want to donate my body   ○ No, I do not want to donate my body

Where I'd like to make my donation (if known, with contact information if applicable):

I want my brain donated for research if I have Alzheimer's disease

○ Yes, I want to donate my brain   ○ No, I do not want to donate my brain

Where I'd like to make my donation (if known, with contact information if applicable):

....

....

....

I want to donate specific organs

○ Yes, I want to donate specific organs   ○ No, I do not want to donate specific organs

Organs I'd like to donate:

....

....

Where I'd like to donate the organs (if known, with contact information if applicable):

....

....

....

I want to donate any needed organs or tissue

○ Yes, I want to donate any needed organs or tissue   ○ No, I do not want to donate any needed organs or tissue

Where I'd like to make my donation (if known, with contact information if applicable):

....

....

....

Specific donor organizations

List and locations of organizations:

....

....

....

....

6 | Cremation or Burial

Whether you choose to be cremated or buried is an entirely personal decision. Many people feel it is up to the living to decide and have no preference. Even without a personal preference, choosing your final resting place in advance can be a loving thing to do as it helps take away the burden of this decision from your family and friends.

To my loved ones:

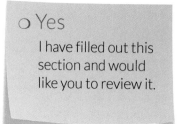

○ Yes
I have filled out this section and would like you to review it.

○ No
I have not provided information as this section is not relevant to me.

I want to be embalmed

○ Yes, I want to be embalmed   ○ No, I do not want to be embalmed

Deed to cemetery plot

○ Yes, I have a deed   ○ No, I don't have a deed

Location of document:

Contact information:

Notes:

Burial insurance

○ Yes, I have burial insurance   ○ No, I don't have burial insurance

Location of document:

Contact information:

Cremation

I want to be cremated: ○ Yes ○ No

I want to be cremated immediately: ○ Yes ○ No

I want to be cremated after my services: ○ Yes ○ No

I want to cremated in the following clothing :

I want you to choose my cremation attire: ○ Yes ○ No

I want my ashes to be placed in an urn: ○ Yes ○ No

I want my ashes to be placed in an urn I have chosen: ○ Yes ○ No

Details:

I want my ashes to be buried: ○ Yes ○ No

I want my ashes to be buried next to:

Details:

I want my ashes to be buried with:

Details:

I want my ashes to be spread: ○ Yes ○ No

I want my ashes to be spread by the following people in the following location(s):

Details:

Burial

I want to be buried: ○ Yes   ○ No

I want to be buried in the following clothing:

....

....

I want you to choose my burial attire: ○ Yes   ○ No

Details:

....

....

I want to be buried in the ground: ○ Yes   ○ No

I want to be buried above ground: ○ Yes   ○ No

I want to be buried next to:

....

Details:

....

....

I want to be buried along with the following persons:

Details:

....

....

I want to be buried with the following items:

Details:

....

....

I want you to choose my casket : ○ Yes   ○ No

I want to be in the following type of casket:

Details:

....

....

Markers

I want a headstone: ○ Yes ○ No

Details:
....

....

I want a grave marker : ○ Yes ○ No

Details:
....

....

I want a monument: ○ Yes ○ No

Details:
....

....

I want a mausoleum: ○ Yes ○ No

Details:
....

....

I want the following inscription:
....

....

I want you to decide my inscription: ○ Yes ○ No

7 | Biographical Data

Organizing all of your essential biographical information in one spot is a great way to help loved ones quickly find the common information they'll be asked for in any number of situations after your death.

Remember to keep this updated as phone numbers and addresses can change.

To my loved ones:

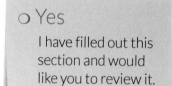

○ Yes
I have filled out this section and would like you to review it.

○ No
I have not provided information as this section is not relevant to me.

About you

Full name:
....

Residential address:
....

....

Mailing address (if different):
....

....

Employer name/company name:
....

Employment address :
....

....

Date of birth:
....

Place of birth:
....

Location of birth certificate:
....

Mobile phone:

Home phone:

Work phone:

Marital status:

Spouse's full name: Spouse's maiden name:

Location of marriage license/certificate:

Children and dependents

List full names, addresses and birth dates:

Parents and stepparents

List names, addresses and birth dates:

Siblings

List names, addresses and birth dates:

_____

_____

_____

_____

_____

_____

_____

Social security number

List Number: _____   Card location: _____

Passport

List Number: _____   Passport location: _____

Driver's license

List number and state: _____   Driver's license location: _____

Military service: ○ Yes   ○ No

Details: _____

_____

Adoption certificate: ○ Yes   ○ No

Location of adoption certificate: _____

_____

Religion

List religion:

Naturalization papers: ○ Yes   ○ No

Location of papers:

Details:

Prior marriages: ○ Yes   ○ No

List date(s) and name(s) of prior marriages:

Divorce, death, or annulment of prior marriages: ○ Yes   ○ No

List dates and details:

Divorce judgment, decree, or stipulation agreement: ○ Yes   ○ No

Location of document(s):

Details:

Child support payments: ○ Yes   ○ No

Location of document(s):

Details:

Alimony settlement payments: ○ Yes ○ No

Location of document(s):
....

Details:
....

Property settlement: ○ Yes ○ No

Location of document(s):
....

Details:
....

Qualified domestic relations order (QDRO): ○ Yes ○ No

Location of document:
....

Details:
....

General power of attorney (finances): ○ Yes ○ No

Contact information:
....

....

Location of document:
....

Details:
....

Copies of power of attorney (finances): ○ Yes ○ No

Location of copies:
....

Details:
....

8 | Obituary

Have you considered writing your own obituary? If you take the time to write your own, you will have control over your life's final message in the end. If you'd prefer your loved ones to do this, this section will help make sure they have the essential information you'd like to have included.

To my loved ones:

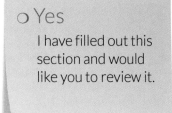

o Yes
I have filled out this section and would like you to review it.

o No
I have not provided information as this section is not relevant to me.

I have written a draft of my obituary: ○ Yes   ○ No

Location of my obituary draft:
....

Person chosen to write or edit my obituary:
....

Contact information:
....

Photograph chosen by me for obituary:
....

Location of photograph:
....

Birth date and place:
....

Marriage date:
....

Choice of charity for donation in lieu of flowers:
....

Contact information:
....

....

Club memberships and contact information:

Community affiliations and contact information:

Education, degrees and honors awarded:

Location of these document(s):

Employment and contact information:

Favorite hobbies:

Important/significant achievements:

Military service (list contact information and location of documents):

National organizations (list contact information and location of documents):

News publication list for obituary (list contact information):

Predeceased family members:

Spouse, children, grandchildren and residences (list contact information):

Volunteer/charitable work (list contact information):

Additional information:

9 Usernames, Passwords & Pin Numbers

Digital assets may be important to access in order to retrieve information, secure your data, or to turn off your accounts. Without the benefit of your usernames and passwords, this becomes a very complex and difficult task for your loved ones.

To my loved ones:

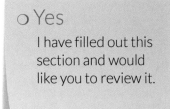

o Yes
I have filled out this section and would like you to review it.

o No
I have not provided information as this section is not relevant to me.

Smartphone: ○ Yes ○ No

Username: .... Password: .... Pin: ....

Blackberry: ○ Yes ○ No

Username: .... Password: .... Pin: ....

Home computer: ○ Yes ○ No

Username: .... Password: .... Pin: ....

iPad(s)/tablets: ○ Yes ○ No

Username: .... Password: .... Pin: ....

Office computer: ○ Yes　○ No

Username: .... Password: .... Pin: ....

Storage devices: ○ Yes　○ No

List: ....

Username: .... Password: .... Pin: ....

List: ....

Username: .... Password: .... Pin: ....

Kindle / Nook / other: ○ Yes　○ No

List: ....

Username: .... Password: .... Pin: ....

Other digital assets: ○ Yes　○ No

List: ....

Username: .... Password: .... Pin: ....

List: ....

Username: .... Password: .... Pin: ....

10 | Funeral & Memorial Services

Many people wonder what the difference is between a funeral and a memorial service. While there are no strict rules and your life should be celebrated in whatever way you choose, traditionally funerals take place with the body or the ashes of the deceased person present. Memorial services are ceremonies without the presence of the body, although an urn containing the ashes may be present. Funerals are usually held immediately following death whereas memorial services may take place weeks or months afterwards. Whatever kind of service you choose, helping your loved ones create a service that honors your life is a true gift to the living.

To my loved ones:

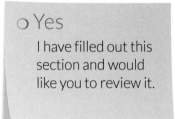

○ Yes
I have filled out this section and would like you to review it.

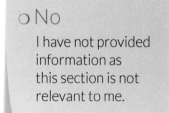

○ No
I have not provided information as this section is not relevant to me.

Funeral service

I want to have a funeral service:

○ Yes   ○ No   ○ No preference (my loved ones may decide on my behalf)

I have planned my funeral service and the information is located:
....

Clergy/officiant/celebrant:
....

Contact information:
....

....

Funeral home:
....

Contact information:
....

Funeral director:
....

Contact Information:
....

Funeral service details

I have made preplanned/prepaid funeral arrangements: ○ Yes   ○ No

Location of documents:
....

Details:
....

....

I want to have a religious service: ○ Yes   ○ No

Details:
....

....

I want to have a military service: ○ Yes   ○ No

Details:
....

....

I want to have a viewing: ○ Yes   ○ No

Details:
....

....

I want to have a wake: ○ Yes   ○ No

Details:
....

....

I want to have calling hours: ○ Yes   ○ No

Details:
....

....

I want to have the following special requests:

....

....

....

....

I want to have my body present: ○ Yes   ○ No

Details:

....

....

I want to have an open casket: ○ Yes   ○ No

Details:

....

....

I want to have a closed casket: ○ Yes   ○ No

Details:

....

....

Participants (include contact information):

....

....

....

....

Ushers (include contact information):

....

....

....

....

Pallbearers (include contact information):

Speaker(s) chosen for my eulogy (include contact information):

Person(s) chosen to read at my funeral service (include contact information):

I want to have specific scripture or literature read: ○ Yes   ○ No

Details:

Favorite music and hymns:

I want to have a soloist sing: ○ Yes   ○ No

Contact information:

I want to have musicians perform: ○ Yes   ○ No

Contact information:

....

....

I want to have a videographer: ○ Yes   ○ No

Contact information:

....

....

I want to have flowers: ○ Yes   ○ No

Contact information:

....

....

Favorite flowers:

....

I have selected photographs for my service: ○ Yes   ○ No

Location of photographs:

....

Details:

....

....

I have selected acknowledgment cards/words of expression: ○ Yes   ○ No

Location of acknowledgment cards/words of expression:

....

Details:

....

....

I want to have an online guest book: ○ Yes   ○ No

I have selected a sign-in book: ○ Yes   ○ No

Location of sign-in book:

....

I want to have a graveside ceremony: ○ Yes   ○ No

Details:

....

....

....

I want to have a reception after to celebrate my life: ○ Yes   ○ No

Location of reception (include contact information):

....

....

Details:

....

....

....

I want to invite the public to the reception: ○ Yes   ○ No

I have made a list of invitees to the reception: ○ Yes   ○ No

Location of list:

....

I have not made a list and only want to invite the following people to the reception (list names and contact information):

....

....

....

....

....

....

Transportation to service (include contact information):

....

....

....

Local hotels for family and guests (include location and contact information):

....

....

....

Additional information:

....

....

....

....

Memorial service

I want to have a memorial service:

○ Yes   ○ No   ○ No preference (my loved ones may decide on my behalf)

I have planned my memorial service and the information is located:

....

Clergy/officiant/celebrant:

....

Contact information:

....

....

....

Memorial service details

I have made preplanned/prepaid memorial service arrangements: ○ Yes   ○ No

Location of documents:

Details:

I want to have a religious service: ○ Yes   ○ No

Details:

I want to have a military service: ○ Yes   ○ No

Details:

Participants (include contact information):

Ushers (include contact information):

Speaker(s) chosen for my eulogy (include contact information):

....

....

....

Person(s) chosen to read at my memorial service (include contact information):

....

....

....

I want to have specific scripture or literature read: ○ Yes   ○ No

Details:

....

....

....

Favorite music and hymns:

....

....

....

I want to have a soloist sing: ○ Yes   ○ No

Contact information:

....

....

I want to have musicians perform: ○ Yes   ○ No

Contact information:

....

....

I want to have a videographer: ○ Yes   ○ No

Contact information:
....

....

I want to have flowers: ○ Yes   ○ No

Contact information:
....

....

Favorite flowers:
....

I have selected photographs for my service: ○ Yes   ○ No

Location of photographs:
....

Details:
....

....

....

I have selected acknowledgment cards/words of expression: ○ Yes   ○ No

Location of acknowledgment cards/words of expression:
....

Details:
....

....

I want to have an online guest book: ○ Yes   ○ No

I have selected a sign-in book: ○ Yes   ○ No

Location of sign-in book:
....

I want to have a reception after to celebrate my life: ○ Yes   ○ No

Location of reception (include contact information):
....

Details:
....

....

I want to invite the public to the reception: ○ Yes   ○ No

I have made a list of invitees to the reception: ○ Yes   ○ No

Location of list:
....

I have not made a list and only want to invite the following people to the reception (list names and contact information):
....

....

....

....

....

....

....

Transportation to service (include contact information):
....

....

....

Local hotels for family and guests (include location and contact information):
....

....

....

Additional information:
....

....

....

....

11 | Pets/Horses/Livestock Exotic Animals

Your pets are important members of your family, so thinking about how to care for them after you die is a loving and essential step.

To my loved ones:

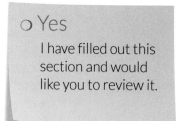

○ Yes
I have filled out this section and would like you to review it.

○ No
I have not provided information as this section is not relevant to me.

Dogs and cats

○ Yes   ○ No

List type, name, and location of dogs and cats:

....

....

....

Veterinarian's contact information:

....

....

Designation of caretaker for pet(s) (include name and contact information):

....

....

Pet insurance

○ Yes   ○ No

List company and contact information:

....

....

....

Fish/aquatics

○ Yes   ○ No

List type, name, and location of fish/aquatics:

....

....

....

Designation of caretaker for fish/aquatics (include name and contact information):

....

....

Horses

○ Yes   ○ No

List type, name, and location of horse(s):

....

....

....

Designation of caretaker for horses (include name and contact information):

....

....

Guinea pig/mice/hamster/rodent

○ Yes   ○ No

List type, name, and location of animal(s):

....

....

....

Designation of caretaker for guinea pig/mice/hamster/rodent (include name and contact information):

....

....

Birds

◯ Yes ◯ No

List type, name, and location of bird(s):

....

....

....

Designation of caretaker for birds (include name and contact information):

....

....

Reptiles/exotic pets

◯ Yes ◯ No

List type, name, and location of reptiles or exotic pets:

....

....

....

Designation of caretaker for reptiles or exotic pets (include name and contact information):

....

....

Livestock

◯ Yes ◯ No

List type, name, and location of livestock:

....

....

Designation of caretaker for livestock (include name and contact information):

....

....

Additional details

....

12 Household and/or Service Providers

List the people and providers you use that your loved ones need to be aware of.

To my loved ones:

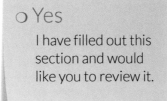

o Yes
I have filled out this section and would like you to review it.

o No
I have not provided information as this section is not relevant to me.

Attorney: ....

Contact information: ....

....

Estate attorney: ....

Contact information: ....

....

Financial advisor: ....

Contact information: ....

....

Tax accountant: ....

Contact information: ....

....

Health care provider(s) (include contact information):

....

....

....

....

Household employee(s) (include contact information):

....

....

....

....

Schools attended by children (include contact information):

....

....

....

....

Other:

....

....

....

....

....

13 | Will and Trusts

Estate planning is an important aspect of expressing your final wishes. This section will help you navigate the items needed to plan your estate.

To my loved ones:

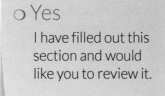

○ Yes
I have filled out this section and would like you to review it.

○ No
I have not provided information as this section is not relevant to me.

I have an estate planning attorney: ○ Yes   ○ No

Contact information:

....

....

....

I have a letter of instruction to my estate attorney: ○ Yes   ○ No

Location of letter:

....

I have other types of attorneys: ○ Yes   ○ No

Contact information:

....

....

....

....

I have executed a last will and testament: ○ Yes ○ No

Contact information:
....

....

....

Location of last will and testament:
....

....

Date last will was executed:
....

Copies of last will are located at:
....

....

Executor's names (include contact information):
....

....

....

I have codicils to my last will: ○ Yes ○ No

I have copies of codicils: ○ Yes ○ No

Location of codicils:
....

I have an ethical will: ○ Yes ○ No

I have copies of my ethical will: ○ Yes ○ No

Location of ethical will:
....

I have a revocable trust: ○ Yes ○ No

I have copies of my revocable trust: ○ Yes ○ No

Location of revocable trust:
....

Trustees' names (include contact information):

I have irrevocable trusts: ○ Yes ○ No

I have copies of irrevocable trusts: ○ Yes ○ No

Location of irrevocable trusts:

Trustees' names (include contact information):

I am a beneficiary of a trust: ○ Yes ○ No

Details (include contact information):

I have a copy of the beneficiary trust(s): ○ Yes ○ No

Location of documents:

I have trusts of which I am a trustee: ○ Yes ○ No

Details (include contact information):

I have trustee records: ○ Yes ○ No

Location of records:

I have charitable remainder trusts: ○ Yes ○ No

I have copies of charitable remainder trusts: ○ Yes ○ No

Location of documents:

I have trusts for minors: ○ Yes ○ No

I have copies of trusts for minors: ○ Yes ○ No

Location of documents:
....

I have Crummey trusts: ○ Yes ○ No

I have copies of Crummey trusts: ○ Yes ○ No

Location of documents:
....

I have a distribution letter of my personal assets: ○ Yes ○ No

Location of distribution letter:
....

I have named guardians for my minor children: ○ Yes ○ No

Contact information:
....

....

....

I have guardianship of another adult: ○ Yes ○ No

Location of documents:
....

Contact Information:
....

....

I am serving as executor of a person's estate: ○ Yes ○ No

Location of documents:
....

Contact information:
....

....

....

14 | Employment

Your loved ones may need to contact your employer and coordinate outstanding issues, benefits, or documents. If you own your own business or are a sole proprietor, you might consider listing your current clients as well to ensure they are notified in the event of your death.

To my loved ones:

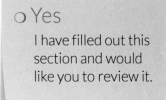

o Yes
I have filled out this section and would like you to review it.

o No
I have not provided information as this section is not relevant to me.

Current employer(s) contact information:

....

....

....

....

Current title and position:

....

....

Ownership interest in business of employment (include contact information):

....

....

....

....

Current partnership relationship (include contact information):

Outstanding bonus, commission, wages (include contact information):

Unreimbursed expenses (include contact information):

Current benefit documents:

Location of benefit documents:

Former employment (include contact information):

....

....

....

....

I have made a list of my current clients: ○ Yes   ○ No

Location of client list:

....

Current clients (include contact information):

....

....

....

....

....

....

....

....

....

....

....

CHAPTER 2

FINANCIAL MATTERS

"The secret of getting ahead

is getting started."

-MARK TWAIN

Instructions for loved ones to help find, manage, secure and/or resolve your finances.

Even if others have always handled your family's finances, your loved ones may be overwhelmed by the number of financial matters they will have to settle in the weeks or months following your death.

This chapter will help walk you through the various aspects of your financial affairs that you will need to get in order.

In this chapter:

Helpful information for your loved ones:

✓ Many financial institutions, government agencies, creditors, unions, membership groups and other organizations won't even talk to your loved ones about your financial affairs let alone take action, like closing an account, until they produce a death certificate.

✓ The first order of business for your loved ones is to go to the city clerk's office or your local vital statistics office and get certified copies of the death certificate. They will need this valuable document before starting to contact banks, investment companies and other firms.

✓ Obtain at least 10 copies of the death certificate; 20 copies would be even better.

1 | Bank Accounts

To my loved ones:

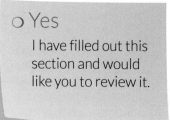

○ Yes
I have filled out this section and would like you to review it.

○ No
I have not provided information as this section is not relevant to me.

Certificates of deposit

○ Yes   ○ No

List accounts, contact information and location of documents:

....

....

....

....

Savings accounts

○ Yes   ○ No

List accounts, contact information and location of documents:

....

....

....

....

Checking accounts

○ Yes   ○ No

List accounts, contact information and location of documents:

....

....

....

....

Passbook accounts

○ Yes   ○ No

List accounts, contact information and location of documents:

....

....

....

....

2 | Brokerage Accounts

To my loved ones:

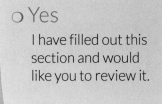

○ Yes
I have filled out this section and would like you to review it.

○ No
I have not provided information as this section is not relevant to me.

Financial advisor/planner

○ Yes   ○ No

Contact information:

Brokerage accounts

○ Yes   ○ No

List accounts, contact information and location of statements:

Money market accounts

○ Yes   ○ No

List accounts and location of documents:

Online access accounts

○ Yes   ○ No

List accounts and location of statements:

....

....

....

Debit card accounts

○ Yes   ○ No

List accounts and location of statements:

....

....

....

Treasury bills

○ Yes   ○ No

List accounts and location of statements:

....

....

....

Treasury bonds

○ Yes   ○ No

List accounts and location of statements:

....

....

....

Municipal bonds

○ Yes   ○ No

List accounts and location of statements:

....

....

....

Corporate bonds

◯ Yes ◯ No

List accounts and location of documents:

....

....

....

Series E bonds

◯ Yes ◯ No

List accounts and location of statements:

....

....

....

Escrow mortgage accounts

◯ Yes ◯ No

List accounts and location of statements:

....

....

....

E-trade accounts

◯ Yes ◯ No

List accounts and location of statements:

....

....

....

3 Safe Deposit Box

To my loved ones:

○ Yes
I have filled out this section and would like you to review it.

○ No
I have not provided information as this section is not relevant to me.

Safe deposit boxes

I have safe deposit boxes: ○ Yes ○ No

List locations:

Safe deposit box contents:

I have a separate list of safe deposit contents: ○ Yes ○ No

Location of list:

Safe deposit box key

○ Yes ○ No

Location of key:

Persons with access to safe deposit box

List names and contact information:

4 | Business Ownership

To my loved ones:

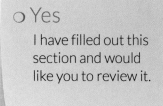

o Yes
I have filled out this section and would like you to review it.

o No
I have not provided information as this section is not relevant to me.

Ownership of business

List contact information and location of documents:

Title of how the business is held

List contact information and location of documents:

Business partners and partnership documents

List contact information and location of documents:

Succession plan document

Location of document:

5 | Insurance

To my loved ones:

○ Yes
I have filled out this section and would like you to review it.

○ No
I have not provided information as this section is not relevant to me.

Life insurance

○ Yes ○ No

List accounts and contact information:

HSA

○ Yes ○ No

List accounts and contact information:

Healthcare

○ Yes ○ No

List accounts and contact information:

Disability

○ Yes ○ No

List accounts and contact information:

Flexible Spending Account

○ Yes ○ No

List accounts and contact information:

Accidental death

○ Yes ○ No

List accounts and contact information:

Dental

○ Yes　○ No

List accounts and contact information:

....

....

....

Auto

○ Yes　○ No

List accounts and contact information:

....

....

....

Homeowner

○ Yes　○ No

List accounts and contact information:

....

....

....

Umbrella

○ Yes　○ No

List accounts and contact information:

....

....

....

Personal liability

○ Yes　○ No

List accounts and contact information:

....

....

....

Rental

○ Yes　○ No

List accounts and contact information:

....

....

....

Long term care

○ Yes　○ No

List accounts and contact information:

....

....

....

Vision

○ Yes　○ No

List accounts and contact information:

....

....

....

Pet

○ Yes　○ No

List accounts and contact information:

....

....

....

Flood

○ Yes　○ No

List accounts and contact information:

....

....

....

Jewelry

○ Yes   ○ No

List accounts and contact information:

TIAA/CREF

○ Yes   ○ No

List accounts and contact information:

Boat

○ Yes   ○ No

List accounts and contact information:

Malpractice

○ Yes   ○ No

List accounts and contact information:

Art

○ Yes   ○ No

List accounts and contact information:

Other

○ Yes   ○ No

List types, accounts and contact information:

6 | Retirement Plans

To my loved ones:

○ Yes
I have filled out this section and would like you to review it.

○ No
I have not provided information as this section is not relevant to me.

IRA (individual retirement account)

○ Yes   ○ No

List accounts (include contact information):

....

....

IRA statement location:

....

Beneficiary designation of IRA (include contact information):

....

....

Roth IRA accounts

○ Yes   ○ No

List accounts (include contact information):

....

....

Roth IRA statement location:

....

Beneficiary designation of Roth IRA (include contact information):

....

....

Company profit sharing plans

○ Yes   ○ No

List accounts (include contact information):

....

....

....

....

Profit sharing statement location:
....

401k accounts

○ Yes   ○ No

List accounts (include contact information):

....

....

....

....

401k statement location:
....

403b account

○ Yes   ○ No

List accounts (include contact information):

....

....

....

....

403b statement location:
....

SEP (Simplified Employee Pension)

○ Yes   ○ No

List accounts (include contact information):

SEP statement location:

Other

○ Yes   ○ No

List accounts (include contact information and statement locations):

7 | Social Security/Pensions/ Government Benefits

To my loved ones:

○ Yes
I have filled out this section and would like you to review it.

○ No
I have not provided information as this section is not relevant to me.

Social security number:

Location of social security card:

Pension

○ Yes ○ No

List accounts (include contact information):

Pension statement location:

Supplemental security income (SSI)

○ Yes ○ No

List accounts (include contact information):

SSI statement location:

Government benefits

○ Yes ○ No

List accounts (include contact information):

Benefits statement location:

Veterans benefits

○ Yes ○ No

List accounts (include contact information):

Benefits statement location:

8 | Debt

To my loved ones:

○ Yes
I have filled out this section and would like you to review it.

○ No
I have not provided information as this section is not relevant to me.

Accountant

Contact information:

Taxes due

○ Yes   ○ No

List status and location of information:

Date and location of last tax return filed:

Estimated taxes due

○ Yes   ○ No

List location of forms:

Gift tax returns

○ Yes   ○ No

Location of documents:

Automated bill payments

○ Yes ○ No

List accounts (include contact information):

Credit cards/charge cards

○ Yes ○ No

List cards (include contact information):

Past due accounts

○ Yes ○ No

List accounts (include contact information):

Home mortgage

○ Yes ○ No

List details (include contact information):

Automobile loans

○ Yes ○ No

List details (include contact information):

Student loans

○ Yes ○ No

List details (include contact information):

Mortgage/home equity loan

○ Yes ○ No

List details (include contact information):

Business loans

○ Yes ○ No

List details (include contact information):

Alimony and child support

○ Yes ○ No

List details (include contact information):

Outstanding pledge to school or charity

○ Yes ○ No

List details (include contact information):

Unsecured loans

○ Yes ○ No

List details (include contact information):

....

....

....

Cosigned debt

○ Yes ○ No

List details (include contact information):

....

....

....

Promissory notes

○ Yes ○ No

List details (include contact information):

....

....

....

Court-ordered payment

○ Yes ○ No

List details (include contact information):

....

....

....

Lawsuit settlements and pending lawsuits

○ Yes ○ No

List details (include contact information):

....

....

....

9 | Other Sources of Income/ Financial Assets

To my loved ones:

o Yes
I have filled out this section and would like you to review it.

o No
I have not provided information as this section is not relevant to me.

I have other sources of income

○ Yes   ○ No

Details:

Cash

○ Yes   ○ No

Details:

Accounts/notes receivable

○ Yes   ○ No

Details:

Debts owed to me or assets on loans to others

○ Yes   ○ No

Details:

Bus/subway/railway passes

○ Yes   ○ No

Details:

Tax refunds

○ Yes   ○ No

Details:

Digital assets

○ Yes   ○ No

Details:

Lottery tickets or online lottery account

○ Yes   ○ No

Details:

Season tickets (sports/theatre/etc.)

○ Yes   ○ No

Details:

Airline club memberships

○ Yes   ○ No

Details:

Intellectual property or patents

○ Yes   ○ No

Details: ....

....

....

Blogs

○ Yes   ○ No

Details: ....

....

....

Unclaimed property/missing property

○ Yes   ○ No

Details: ....

....

....

Unused airline tickets

○ Yes   ○ No

Details: ....

....

....

Pending lawsuits

○ Yes   ○ No

Details: ....

....

....

Other

○ Yes   ○ No

Details: ....

....

....

10 | Promissory Notes/ Royalties/Annuity Contracts

To my loved ones:

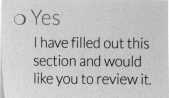

○ Yes
I have filled out this section and would like you to review it.

○ No
I have not provided information as this section is not relevant to me.

Promissory notes owed to me

○ Yes   ○ No

List contact information and location of documents:

....

....

....

Royalties

○ Yes   ○ No

List contact information and location of documents:

....

....

....

Annuity contracts

○ Yes   ○ No

List contact information and location of documents:

....

....

....

11 | Assets Held in Another State or Country

To my loved ones:

○ **Yes**
I have filled out this section and would like you to review it.

○ **No**
I have not provided information as this section is not relevant to me.

Accounts

○ Yes ○ No

List contact information and details:

....

....

Location of documents:

....

Assets

○ Yes ○ No

List contact information and details:

....

....

Location of documents:

....

Formerly owned real estate

○ Yes ○ No

List contact information and details:

....

....

Location of documents:

....

CHAPTER 3

REAL ESTATE MATTERS

*"I try to just communicate
what I want done as clearly
and simply as possible."*

–DICK WOLF

Instructions for loved ones to help them manage and/or maintain your real estate.

This chapter will walk you through the items you need to consider in order to help your loved ones care for, manage, maintain, sell or distribute your real estate holdings, including land, rental properties and lease agreements, and commercial and personal properties.

In this chapter:

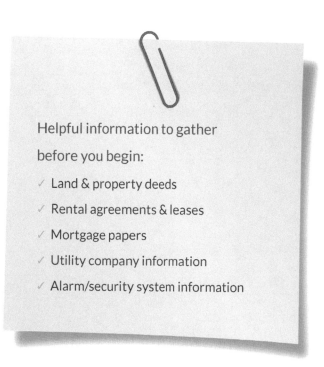

Helpful information to gather

before you begin:

✓ Land & property deeds

✓ Rental agreements & leases

✓ Mortgage papers

✓ Utility company information

✓ Alarm/security system information

1 Real Estate Located in United States

To my loved ones:

○ **Yes**
I have filled out this section and would like you to review it.

○ **No**
I have not provided information as this section is not relevant to me.

Property address and location of keys:

....

....

Maintenance providers' contact information:

....

....

....

....

Title of property (joint or individual) : ....

Location of documents: ....

Location of original deed: ....

Mortgage company

○ Yes   ○ No

Contact information:

....

....

Location of original mortgage document:

....

Title insurance document

○ Yes　○ No

Contact information:
....
....

Location of title insurance document:
....

Property easements

○ Yes　○ No

List easements and location of documents:
....
....
....

Alarm system company contact information:
....

Alarm code or alarm password:
....
....

Caretaker/housekeeper contact information:
....
....

Landscaper/gardener contact information:
....
....

Water meter location:
....

Well

○ Yes　○ No

Contact information:
....
....

Oil

○ Yes   ○ No

Contact information:

....

....

Oil tank refuel access location:

....

Prepaid oil contract details:

....

....

Gas/electric

○ Yes   ○ No

Gas and electric company contact information:

....

....

Septic tank

○ Yes   ○ No

Septic company contact information:

....

....

Propane tank

○ Yes   ○ No

Propane gas tank company contact information:

....

....

Generator

○ Yes   ○ No

Generator service contract contact information:

....

....

Other

Cable/television provider contact information:

Locksmith to secure home after death contact information:

List of trusted neighbors contact information:

Location of warranty information for property:

Time share property

○ Yes   ○ No

List property contact information:

Location of time share documents and keys to property:

Property rented by me

○ Yes   ○ No

List property location and landlord contact information:

Location of rental agreement document and keys to property:

Property rented to others

◯ Yes   ◯ No

List property location and lessee contact information:

....

....

....

Location of rental property agreement and keys to rental property:

....

Commercial property

◯ Yes   ◯ No

List property, contact information, and location of keys:

....

....

Continual Care Retirement Community (CCRC)

◯ Yes   ◯ No

List property, contact information, and location of keys:

....

....

Undeveloped land

◯ Yes   ◯ No

List property and contact information:

....

....

Location of undeveloped land title and deed:

....

Instructions for care of my owned property (list properties):

....

....

....

2 | Real Estate Located Outside the United States

To my loved ones:

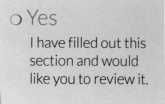

○ Yes
I have filled out this section and would like you to review it.

○ No
I have not provided information as this section is not relevant to me.

Property address and location of keys:
....
....

Maintenance providers contact information:
....
....
....
....

Title of property (joint or individual) :
....

Location of documents:
....

Location of original deed:
....

Mortgage company

○ Yes   ○ No

Contact information:
....
....

Location of original mortgage document:

Title insurance document

○ Yes   ○ No

Contact information:
....

....

Location of title insurance document:
....

Property easements

○ Yes   ○ No

List easements and location of documents:
....

....

....

Alarm system company contact information:
....

Alarm code or alarm password:
....

Caretaker/housekeeper contact information:
....

....

Landscaper/gardener contact information:
....

....

Water meter location:
....

Well

○ Yes   ○ No

Contact information:
....

....

Oil

○ Yes　○ No

Contact information:

Oil tank refuel access location:

Prepaid oil contract details:

Gas/electric

○ Yes　○ No

Gas and electric company contact information:

Septic tank

○ Yes　○ No

Septic company contact information:

Propane tank

○ Yes　○ No

Propane gas tank company contact information:

Generator

○ Yes　○ No

Generator service contract contact information:

Other

Cable/television provider contact information:

....

....

Locksmith to secure home after death contact information:

....

....

List of trusted neighbors contact information:

....

....

....

Location of warranty information for property:

....

Time share property

○ Yes   ○ No

List property contact information:

....

....

Location of time share documents and keys to property:

....

Property rented by me

○ Yes   ○ No

List property location and landlord contact information:

....

....

....

Location of rental agreement document and keys to property:

....

....

Property rented to others

○ Yes   ○ No

List property location and lessee contact information:

....

....

....

Location of rental property agreement and keys to rental property:

....

Commercial property

○ Yes   ○ No

List property, contact information, and location of keys:

....

....

Continual Care Retirement Community (CCRC)

○ Yes   ○ No

List property, contact information, and location of keys:

....

....

Undeveloped land

○ Yes   ○ No

List property and contact information:

....

....

Location of undeveloped land title and deed:

....

Instructions for care of my owned property (list properties):

....

....

....

CHAPTER 4

PERSONAL PROPERTY MATTERS

"The ability to simplify means to eliminate the unnecessary so that the necessary may speak."

– HANS HOFMANN

Instructions for loved ones on how to find, distribute, care for, or maintain your personal property.

Your personal belongings often mean a great deal not only to you, but to those who are left behind after your death. Even the smallest items can become meaningful keepsakes to friends and loved ones. Your loved ones should contact your attorney prior to distributing any property in order to make sure that your estate is handled properly.

This chapter will help prompt you to think about all the various items in your possession that may need to be distributed, cared for, stored, donated or disposed of upon your death.

In this chapter:

1. Computers and Electronics
2. Jewelry
3. Photos, Film, Movies, Slides and Audio tapes
4. Vehicles
5. Club Memberships
6. Tools
7. Cameras
8. Instruments
9. Recreational/Fitness
10. Art
11. Home Safe
12. Bikes
13. Collections
14. Wine
15. Guns/Weapons
16. Frequent Flyer Mileage Accounts
17. Storage Units
18. Unpublished Works/Written Drafts/Notes
19. Boats
20. Airplanes

Helpful information to think about before you begin:

✓ Get family members and friends to help distribute your personal belongings by asking them what they would like after your death

✓ Pass out stickers to your friends and family, and have them put their names on the back of the items they choose

✓ Make a distribution list to avoid potential family disagreements

✓ Consider distributing items while you are still living

✓ Make arrangements for a charitable donation of belongings that aren't designated to a family member

1 Computers and Electronics

To my loved ones:

○ Yes
I have filled out this section and would like you to review it.

○ No
I have not provided information as this section is not relevant to me.

Computers and laptops

○ Yes   ○ No

List and location of computers:

iPhone/BlackBerry/cell phone

○ Yes   ○ No

List and location of smartphone(s):

iPads/tablets

○ Yes   ○ No

List and location of iPads/tablets:

iPod/mp3 player(s)

○ Yes   ○ No

List and location of iPod/mp3 player(s):

Printers/scanners/peripherals

○ Yes   ○ No

List and location of equipment:

....

....

....

....

Televisions and DVRs

○ Yes   ○ No

List and location of television(s):

....

....

....

....

Servers

○ Yes   ○ No

List and location of server(s):

....

....

....

....

Speakers, stereos, music systems

○ Yes   ○ No

List and location of equipment:

....

....

....

....

I wish to transfer computers and electronics upon my death as follows:

Details and contact information:

....

....

....

....

....

....

2 | Jewelry

To my loved ones:

○ Yes
I have filled out this section and would like you to review it.

○ No
I have not provided information as this section is not relevant to me.

Watch(es)

○ Yes   ○ No

Location of watch(es):

....

....

....

....

Insured jewelry

○ Yes   ○ No

Location of jewelry:

....

....

....

Location of insurance documents:

....

....

Wedding ring(s)

○ Yes   ○ No

Location of wedding ring(s):

....

....

....

....

Non-insured jewelry

○ Yes   ○ No

Location of non-insured jewelry:

....

....

....

....

I have a jewelry distribution list

○ Yes   ○ No

Location of distribution list:

....

....

....

....

....

I have jewelry appraisals

○ Yes   ○ No

Location of jewelery appraisals:

....

....

....

....

....

I wish to transfer jewelry upon my death as follows:

Details and contact information:

....

....

....

....

....

....

3 | Photos, Film, Movies, Slides and Audiotapes

To my loved ones:

○ Yes
I have filled out this section and would like you to review it.

○ No
I have not provided information as this section is not relevant to me.

Photo albums

○ Yes   ○ No

Location of photo albums:

....

....

....

....

Historical photos

○ Yes   ○ No

Location of historical photos:

....

....

....

....

Family portraits

○ Yes   ○ No

Location of family portraits:

....

....

....

....

Individual photos

○ Yes   ○ No

Location of individual photos:

....

....

....

....

Digital photos

○ Yes   ○ No

Location of digital photos:

Negatives/film

○ Yes   ○ No

Location of negatives/film:

Movies and/or videos

○ Yes   ○ No

Location of movies and/or videos:

Audiotapes

○ Yes   ○ No

Location of audiotapes:

I wish to transfer photos/film/etc. upon my death as follows:

Details and contact information:

4 Vehicles

To my loved ones:

○ Yes
I have filled out this section and would like you to review it.

○ No
I have not provided information as this section is not relevant to me.

Automobiles, trucks and titles

○ Yes   ○ No

List and location of vehicles:

....

....

....

....

....

Location of titles:

....

....

Service documents

Location of documents:

....

....

....

Vehicle loan/creditor

○ Yes   ○ No

List (include contact information):

....

....

....

Location of documents:

....

....

Leased vehicles and leaseholder

○ Yes   ○ No

Contact information:

....

....

....

Location of documents:

....

....

All-terrain vehicles (ATV) and titles

○ Yes ○ No

List and location of ATVs:

Location of titles:

Farm vehicles and titles

○ Yes ○ No

List and location of farm vehicles:

Location of titles:

Recreational vehicles (RTV) and titles

○ Yes ○ No

List and location of recreational vehicles:

Location of titles:

Campers and titles

○ Yes ○ No

List and location of campers:

Location of titles:

Motorcycles and titles

○ Yes ○ No

List and location of motorcycles:

Location of titles:

Trailers and titles

○ Yes ○ No

List and location of trailers:

Location of titles:

Golf carts and titles

○ Yes   ○ No

List and location of golf carts:

....

....

....

....

Location of titles:

....

....

Electric scooters

○ Yes   ○ No

List and location of scooters:

....

....

....

....

Location of titles:

....

....

I wish to transfer vehicles upon my death as follows:

Details and contact information:

....

....

....

....

....

....

5 | Club Memberships

To my loved ones:

○ Yes
I have filled out this section and would like you to review it.

○ No
I have not provided information as this section is not relevant to me.

Club names and addresses:

....

....

....

....

....

....

....

....

....

....

Location of club ownership documents:

....

6 Tools

To my loved ones:

○ Yes
I have filled out this section and would like you to review it.

○ No
I have not provided information as this section is not relevant to me.

Power tools

○ Yes   ○ No

Location of power tools:

....

....

....

Lawn mowers

○ Yes   ○ No

Location of lawn mowers:

....

....

....

Tool collection

○ Yes   ○ No

Location of tool collection:

....

....

....

Snow thrower

○ Yes   ○ No

Location of snow throwers:

....

....

....

I wish to transfer tools upon my death as follows:

Details and contact information:

....

....

....

....

7 | Cameras

To my loved ones:

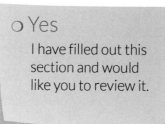

○ Yes
I have filled out this section and would like you to review it.

○ No
I have not provided information as this section is not relevant to me.

Digital cameras

○ Yes   ○ No

Location of cameras:

....

....

....

Video and movie cameras

○ Yes   ○ No

Location of cameras:

....

....

....

Still cameras

○ Yes   ○ No

Location of cameras:

....

....

....

Camcorders

○ Yes   ○ No

Location of camcorders:

....

....

....

I wish to transfer cameras upon my death as follows:

Details and contact information:

....

....

....

....

....

8 | Instruments

To my loved ones:

○ **Yes**
I have filled out this section and would like you to review it.

○ **No**
I have not provided information as this section is not relevant to me.

Guitar

○ Yes   ○ No

Location of guitars:

....

....

....

Piano

○ Yes   ○ No

Location of pianos:

....

....

....

Keyboards

○ Yes   ○ No

Location of keyboards:

....

....

....

String instrument

○ Yes   ○ No

Location of string instruments:

....

....

....

Brass instrument

○ Yes   ○ No

Location of brass instruments:

....

....

....

Woodwind instrument

○ Yes   ○ No

Location of woodwind instruments:

....

....

....

Percussion

○ Yes   ○ No

Location of percussion instruments:
....
....
....

Music studio/recording equipment

○ Yes   ○ No

Location of music studio/recording equipment:
....
....
....

Electrophones

○ Yes   ○ No

Location of electrophones:
....
....
....

Other

○ Yes   ○ No

List and location:
....
....
....

I wish to transfer instruments upon my death as follows:

Details and contact information:
....
....
....
....
....
....

9 | Recreational/Fitness

To my loved ones:

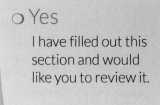

o Yes
I have filled out this section and would like you to review it.

o No
I have not provided information as this section is not relevant to me.

Golf clubs

○ Yes   ○ No

Location of golf clubs:

Ski/snowboard equipment

○ Yes   ○ No

Location of ski/snowboard equipment:

Tennis racquets

○ Yes   ○ No

Location of tennis racquets:

Camping gear

○ Yes   ○ No

Location of camping gear:

Biking equipment

○ Yes   ○ No

Location of biking equipment:

Hockey equipment

○ Yes   ○ No

Location of hockey equipment:

Playground equipment

○ Yes   ○ No

Location of playground equipment:

Baseball equipment

○ Yes   ○ No

Location of baseball equipment:

Snowmobiles

○ Yes ○ No

Location of snowmobiles:

....

....

Scuba/snorkel

○ Yes ○ No

Location of equipment:

....

....

Pool table/ping pong

○ Yes ○ No

Location of equipment:

....

....

Treadmill/elliptical/recumbent bike

○ Yes ○ No

Location of equipment:

....

....

Lacrosse equipment

○ Yes ○ No

Location of equipment:

....

....

Stationary bike/gym weights

○ Yes ○ No

Location of equipment:

....

....

Canoes/kayaks

○ Yes ○ No

Location of canoes/kayaks:

....

....

Surfboards

○ Yes ○ No

Location of surfboards:

....

....

Windsurfing/kite boarding

○ Yes ○ No

Location of equipment:

....

....

Boogie boards/tubing tubes

○ Yes ○ No

Location of equipment:

....

....

Fishing

○ Yes ○ No

Location of fishing equipment:

....

....

Water skis/wakeboards

○ Yes ○ No

Location of water sports equipment:

....

....

Jet skis

○ Yes   ○ No

Location of jet skis:

....

....

Trampoline

○ Yes   ○ No

Location of trampoline:

....

....

Skateboards/rollerblades/scooters

○ Yes   ○ No

Location of equipment:

....

....

Other

○ Yes   ○ No

List and location of equipment:

....

....

....

....

I wish to transfer sporting equipment upon my death as follows:

Details and contact information:

....

....

....

....

....

....

10 | Art

To my loved ones:

○ **Yes**
I have filled out this section and would like you to review it.

○ **No**
I have not provided information as this section is not relevant to me.

Fine art

○ Yes   ○ No

List and location of art:

....

....

....

....

Landscape

○ Yes   ○ No

List and location of art:

....

....

....

....

Sculptures

○ Yes   ○ No

List and location of art:

....

....

....

....

Ceramics

○ Yes   ○ No

List and location of art:

....

....

....

....

Quality photographs

○ Yes   ○ No

List and location of art:

....

....

....

....

Religious

○ Yes   ○ No

List and location of art:

....

....

....

....

Folk

◯ Yes ◯ No

List and location of art:

....

....

....

Glass

◯ Yes ◯ No

List and location of art:

....

....

....

Pop art

◯ Yes ◯ No

List and location of art:

....

....

....

Tribal

◯ Yes ◯ No

List and location of art:

....

....

....

Art deco

◯ Yes ◯ No

List and location of art:

....

....

....

Modern

◯ Yes ◯ No

List and location of art:

....

....

....

Primitive

◯ Yes ◯ No

List and location of art:

....

....

....

Poster

◯ Yes ◯ No

List and location of art:

....

....

....

Children's

○ Yes   ○ No

List and location of art:

....

....

....

....

Miniature/wearable

○ Yes   ○ No

List and location of art:

....

....

....

....

Art appraisals

○ Yes   ○ No

List and location of appraised art:

....

....

....

....

....

Location of appraisals:

....

....

....

I wish to transfer art collections upon my death as follows:

Details and contact information:

....

....

....

....

....

....

11 | Home Safe

To my loved ones:

○ **Yes**
I have filled out this section and would like you to review it.

○ **No**
I have not provided information as this section is not relevant to me.

Home safes

○ Yes ○ No

List and location of safes:

....

....

....

Home safe content:

....

....

....

....

....

....

Safe keys

○ Yes ○ No

List and location of keys:

....

....

....

Safe combinations

○ Yes   ○ No

List combinations:

....

....

....

Safe passwords

○ Yes   ○ No

List passwords:

....

....

....

Safe room

○ Yes   ○ No

Location of room:

....

Safe room content:

....

....

....

Safe room access:

....

I wish to transfer safe contents upon my death as follows:

Details and contact information:

....

....

....

12 | Bikes

To my loved ones:

○ **Yes**
I have filled out this section and would like you to review it.

○ **No**
I have not provided information as this section is not relevant to me.

Road

○ Yes ○ No

List and location of bikes and equipment:

....

....

....

....

....

Mountain

○ Yes ○ No

List and location of bikes and equipment:

....

....

....

....

....

Touring

○ Yes ○ No

List and location of bikes and equipment:

....

....

....

....

....

Off-road

○ Yes ○ No

List and location of bikes and equipment:

....

....

....

....

....

Children's

○ Yes   ○ No

List and location of bikes and equipment:

_____

_____

_____

_____

Motorized or electric

○ Yes   ○ No

List and location of bikes and equipment:

_____

_____

_____

_____

BMX or cruiser

○ Yes   ○ No

List and location of bikes and equipment:

_____

_____

_____

_____

Folding or tandem

○ Yes   ○ No

List and location of bikes and equipment:

_____

_____

_____

_____

I wish to transfer bikes upon my death as follows:

Details and contact information:

_____

_____

_____

_____

_____

13 | Collections

To my loved ones:

○ Yes
I have filled out this section and would like you to review it.

○ No
I have not provided information as this section is not relevant to me.

Coins

○ Yes   ○ No

Location of collection:

....

....

....

Paper money

○ Yes   ○ No

Location of collection:

....

....

....

Stamps

○ Yes   ○ No

Location of collection:

....

....

....

Foreign currency

○ Yes   ○ No

Location of collection:

....

....

....

Antiques

○ Yes   ○ No

Location of collection:

....

....

....

Recipes

○ Yes   ○ No

Location of collection:

....

....

....

Games and game systems

○ Yes   ○ No

Location of collection:

CDs/DVDs

○ Yes   ○ No

Location of collection:

Postcards

○ Yes   ○ No

Location of collection:

Dolls/toys

○ Yes   ○ No

Location of collection:

Art

○ Yes   ○ No

Location of collection:

Cars

○ Yes   ○ No

Location of collection:

Silver/gold

○ Yes   ○ No

Location of collection:

Sports memorabilia

○ Yes   ○ No

Location of collection:

Autographs

○ Yes   ○ No

List and location of collection:

Trading cards

○ Yes   ○ No

List and location of collection:

Quilts

○ Yes   ○ No

List and location of collection:

....

....

....

Action figures/comics

○ Yes   ○ No

List and location of collection:

....

....

....

Clothing/shoes

○ Yes   ○ No

List and location of collection:

....

....

....

Pocket knives/weapons

○ Yes   ○ No

List and location of collection:

....

....

....

Record albums/45s

○ Yes   ○ No

List and location of collection:

....

....

....

Other

○ Yes   ○ No

List and location of collection:

....

....

....

I wish to transfer collections upon my death as follows:

Details and contact information:

....

....

....

....

....

....

14 | Wine

To my loved ones:

○ Yes
I have filled out this section and would like you to review it.

○ No
I have not provided information as this section is not relevant to me.

Red

○ Yes   ○ No

Details and location of wine:

White

○ Yes   ○ No

Details and location of wine:

Rose

○ Yes   ○ No

Details and location of wine:

Champagne or sparkling

○ Yes   ○ No

Details and location of champagne:

Dessert wine

○ Yes   ○ No

Details and location of wine:

Fortified/port/marsala

○ Yes   ○ No

Details and location of wine:

I wish to transfer wine upon my death as follows:

Details and contact information:

15 Guns/Weapons

To my loved ones:

○ Yes
I have filled out this section and would like you to review it.

○ No
I have not provided information as this section is not relevant to me.

Warning: my weapons are armed ○ Yes ○ No

Guns are in a safe

○ Yes ○ No

List and location:

....

....

....

....

....

Guns/weapons safe key ○ Yes ○ No

Location of key:

....

Guns/weapons safe combination ○ Yes ○ No

List combination:

....

Guns/weapons safe password ○ Yes ○ No

List password:

....

Ammunition

○ Yes　○ No

Location of ammunition:

....

....

....

Other weapons

○ Yes　○ No

List and location of weapons:

....

....

....

....

....

....

....

....

I wish to transfer guns and weapons upon my death as follows:

Details and contact information:

....

....

....

....

....

16 | Frequent Flyer Mileage Accounts

To my loved ones:

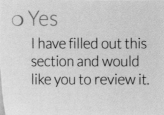

○ **Yes**
I have filled out this section and would like you to review it.

○ **No**
I have not provided information as this section is not relevant to me.

Air Canada

○ Yes ○ No

Account numbers and contact information:

American Eagle

○ Yes ○ No

Account numbers and contact information:

Alaska Airlines

○ Yes ○ No

Account numbers and contact information:

American/US Airways

○ Yes ○ No

Account numbers and contact information:

Allegiant Air

○ Yes ○ No

Account numbers and contact information:

Delta Airlines

○ Yes ○ No

Account numbers and contact information:

Executive Airlines

○ Yes ○ No

Account numbers and contact information:

Southwest Airlines

○ Yes ○ No

Account numbers and contact information:

Frontier Airlines

○ Yes ○ No

Account numbers and contact information:

United Airlines

○ Yes ○ No

Account numbers and contact information:

Hawaiian

○ Yes ○ No

Account numbers and contact information:

Virgin America

○ Yes ○ No

Account numbers and contact information:

JetBlue Airways

○ Yes ○ No

Account numbers and contact information:

Other airline

○ Yes ○ No

Account numbers and contact information:

I wish to transfer frequent flyer mileage accounts upon my death as follows:

Details and contact information:

17 | Storage Units

To my loved ones:

○ **Yes**
I have filled out this section and would like you to review it.

○ **No**
I have not provided information as this section is not relevant to me.

Storage units

○ Yes   ○ No

Location and content of storage units (include contact information):

....

....

....

....

....

....

I wish to transfer contents of storage units upon my death as follows:

Details and contact information:

....

....

....

....

18 | Unpublished Works/ Written Drafts/Notes

To my loved ones:

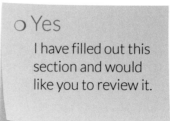

○ Yes
I have filled out this section and would like you to review it.

○ No
I have not provided information as this section is not relevant to me.

Books

○ Yes   ○ No

List and location of books:

....

....

....

Research and/or scientific manuals

○ Yes   ○ No

List and location of documents:

....

....

....

Articles

○ Yes   ○ No

List and location of documents:

....

....

....

Other

○ Yes   ○ No

List and location of documents:

....

....

....

I wish to transfer unpublished works, written drafts and notes upon my death as follows:

Details and contact information:

....

....

....

....

....

19 | Boats

To my loved ones:

○ **Yes**
I have filled out this section and would like you to review it.

○ **No**
I have not provided information as this section is not relevant to me.

Power boat

○ Yes   ○ No

Location of power boats:
....
....
....

Kayaks, rowboats and canoes

○ Yes   ○ No

Location of kayaks, rowboats and canoes:
....
....
....

Sailboat

○ Yes   ○ No

Location of sailboats:
....
....
....

Storage of boats

○ Yes   ○ No

Location (include contact information):
....
....
....

I wish to transfer boats upon my death as follows:

Details and contact information:
....
....
....
....
....

20 | Airplanes

To my loved ones:

○ Yes
I have filled out this section and would like you to review it.

○ No
I have not provided information as this section is not relevant to me.

Airplane/jet

○ Yes　○ No

Details and location of airplane and/or jet:

....

....

Prop plane/biplane

○ Yes　○ No

Details and location of planes:

....

....

Helicopter

○ Yes　○ No

Details and location of helicopters:

....

....

I wish to transfer airplanes upon my death as follows:

Details and contact information:

....

....

....

....

CHAPTER 5

PRIVATE MATTERS

*"Genius is the ability
to put into effect what
is on your mind."*

– F. SCOTT FITZGERALD

Instructions for loved ones about personal, sentimental, private and family matters.

No two people and no two families are alike, and there is clearly no "one size fits all" solution to communicating what matters to you.

This chapter is designed to help you think about the kinds of things you normally don't have to (or choose to) talk about. It's designed to help you communicate about private matters and help loved ones understand the personal places, items and traditions that have been important to you.

In this chapter:

Helpful information to think about before you begin:

✓ Gather a list of your most frequently visited online sites (your browser history will help!)

✓ Brainstorm a list of all the traditions that have meant something to your family

✓ Make a list of all the places things may be "stored" (Boxes? Attics? Dresser drawers? Safe deposit box? Storage lockers?)

✓ Gather together all the keys you have. Is it clear what each one belongs to? Label them.

1 | Digital Accounts

To my loved ones:

○ Yes
I have filled out this section and would like you to review it.

○ No
I have not provided information as this section is not relevant to me.

Financial

| ATM | ○ Yes ○ No | Username: | Password: |

| Online banking | ○ Yes ○ No | Name of institution: | |
| | | Username: | Password: |

| Financial accts online | ○ Yes ○ No | Name of institution: | |
| | | Username: | Password: |

| E-trade | ○ Yes ○ No | Username: | Password: |

| Mint.com | ○ Yes ○ No | Username: | Password: |

| Online storage | ○ Yes ○ No | Username: | Password: |

| Paypal | ○ Yes ○ No | Username: | Password: |

| Other: | | Username: | Password: |

| Other: | | Username: | Password: |

Phones

iPhone   ◯ Yes   ◯ No   Password:

Android   ◯ Yes   ◯ No   Password:

Home phone   ◯ Yes   ◯ No   Password:

Smartphone   ◯ Yes   ◯ No   Password:

Other: Password:

Professional

Work computer   ◯ Yes   ◯ No   Username: Password:

Work apps   ◯ Yes   ◯ No   Name of app:

Username: Password:

iCloud   ◯ Yes   ◯ No   Username: Password:

Gmail   ◯ Yes   ◯ No   Username: Password:

Hotmail   ◯ Yes   ◯ No   Username: Password:

Yahoo!   ◯ Yes   ◯ No   Username: Password:

LinkedIn   ◯ Yes   ◯ No   Username: Password:

Evernote   ◯ Yes   ◯ No   Username: Password:

Blogs   ◯ Yes   ◯ No   URL:

Username: Password:

DNS services   ○ Yes   ○ No   Service name:

Username: Password:

Domains   ○ Yes   ○ No   Domain registrar:

Username: Password:

File sharing   ○ Yes   ○ No   Service name:

Username: Password:

Software licenses   ○ Yes   ○ No   Service name:

Username: Password:

Tax preparation   ○ Yes   ○ No   Service name:

Username: Password:

Web hosting   ○ Yes   ○ No   Service name:

Username: Password:

Other   ○ Yes   ○ No   Service name:

Username: Password:

URL(s)   ○ Yes   ○ No

URL address: .... Username: .... Password: ....

URL address: .... Username: .... Password: ....

URL address: .... Username: .... Password: ....

URL address: .... Username: .... Password: ....

Photo sharing

Instagram   ○ Yes   ○ No   Username: .... Password: ....

Flickr   ○ Yes   ○ No   Username: .... Password: ....

Photobucket   ○ Yes   ○ No   Username: .... Password: ....

Tinypic   ○ Yes   ○ No   Username: .... Password: ....

Shutterfly   ○ Yes   ○ No   Username: .... Password: ....

Snapfish   ○ Yes   ○ No   Username: .... Password: ....

Fotki   ○ Yes   ○ No   Username: .... Password: ....

Picassa Albums   ○ Yes   ○ No   Username: .... Password: ....

Other: .... Username: .... Password: ....

Other: .... Username: .... Password: ....

Other: .... Username: .... Password: ....

Social

Facebook	○ Yes ○ No	Username:	Password:
Twitter	○ Yes ○ No	Username:	Password:
LinkedIn	○ Yes ○ No	Username:	Password:
Google +	○ Yes ○ No	Username:	Password:
Pinterest	○ Yes ○ No	Username:	Password:
YouTube	○ Yes ○ No	Username:	Password:
Tumblr	○ Yes ○ No	Username:	Password:
VK	○ Yes ○ No	Username:	Password:
Instagram	○ Yes ○ No	Username:	Password:
MySpace	○ Yes ○ No	Username:	Password:
FourSquare	○ Yes ○ No	Username:	Password:
Reddit	○ Yes ○ No	Username:	Password:
Tagged	○ Yes ○ No	Username:	Password:
MeetMe	○ Yes ○ No	Username:	Password:
MeetUp	○ Yes ○ No	Username:	Password:
Classmates	○ Yes ○ No	Username:	Password:
Skype	○ Yes ○ No	Username:	Password:
iTunes	○ Yes ○ No	Username:	Password:

Dating sites

Zoosk ○ Yes ○ No Username: Password:

Match.com ○ Yes ○ No Username: Password:

eHarmony ○ Yes ○ No Username: Password:

OurTime ○ Yes ○ No Username: Password:

Christian Mingle ○ Yes ○ No Username: Password:

Other sites

AARP ○ Yes ○ No Username: Password:

Ancestry ○ Yes ○ No Username: Password:

Dropbox ○ Yes ○ No Username: Password:

FamilyTreeMaker ○ Yes ○ No Username: Password:

Plaxo ○ Yes ○ No Username: Password:

Other: Username: Password:

Other: Username: Password:

Other: Username: Password:

Other: Username: Password:

Other: Username: Password:

Other: Username: Password:

Other: Username: Password:

On-line shopping

Amazon	○ Yes ○ No	Username:	Password:
Apple	○ Yes ○ No	Username:	Password:
Barnes & Noble	○ Yes ○ No	Username:	Password:
Best Buy	○ Yes ○ No	Username:	Password:
Ebay	○ Yes ○ No	Username:	Password:
Etsy	○ Yes ○ No	Username:	Password:
Groupon	○ Yes ○ No	Username:	Password:
Home Depot	○ Yes ○ No	Username:	Password:
Ikea	○ Yes ○ No	Username:	Password:
Overstock	○ Yes ○ No	Username:	Password:
Target	○ Yes ○ No	Username:	Password:
Walmart	○ Yes ○ No	Username:	Password:
Zappos	○ Yes ○ No	Username:	Password:
Other:		Username:	Password:
Other:		Username:	Password:
Other:		Username:	Password:
Other:		Username:	Password:
Other:		Username:	Password:

Hotel Accounts

Hotel name:

Account number: Details:

Hotel name:

Account number: Details:

Hotel name:

Account number: Details:

Hotel name:

Account number: Details:

Rental cars

Rental car service name:

Account number: Details:

Rental car service name:

Account number: Details:

Rental car service name:

Account number: Details:

Rental car service name:

Account number: Details:

2 | Bucket List

To my loved ones:

○ Yes
I have filled out this section and would like you to review it.

○ No
I have not provided information as this section is not relevant to me.

I have a Bucket List:

○ Yes   ○ No

Details:

Location of paperwork:

3 | Genealogy

To my loved ones:

○ Yes
I have filled out this section and would like you to review it.

○ No
I have not provided information as this section is not relevant to me.

Details:

Location of documents or other paperwork:

Websites

Ancestry.com ○ Yes ○ No Username: Password:

Archives.com ○ Yes ○ No Username: Password:

4 | Family and Holiday Traditions

To my loved ones:

o Yes
I have filled out this section and would like you to review it.

o No
I have not provided information as this section is not relevant to me.

Details:

_____

_____

_____

_____

_____

_____

_____

_____

_____

Location of documents or other paperwork:

_____

_____

_____

5 | Hidden Assets and Documents

To my loved ones:

○ Yes
I have filled out this section and would like you to review it.

○ No
I have not provided information as this section is not relevant to me.

Details:

Location of documents or other paperwork:

6 | History and/or Photos of Inherited Pieces

To my loved ones:

o Yes
I have filled out this section and would like you to review it.

o No
I have not provided information as this section is not relevant to me.

Details:

Location of documents and other paperwork:

I wish to transfer these documents and paperwork upon my death as follows:

Details and contact information:

7 | Post Office Boxes and Items Stored Elsewhere

To my loved ones:

○ Yes
I have filled out this section and would like you to review it.

○ No
I have not provided information as this section is not relevant to me.

Details:

Location of documents and other paperwork:

I wish to transfer these items upon my death as follows:

Details and contact information:

8 | Other Unusual Documents

To my loved ones:

o Yes
I have filled out this
section and would
like you to review it.

o No
I have not provided
information as
this section is not
relevant to me.

Details:

....

....

....

....

....

....

....

Location of documents:

....

....

I wish to transfer these documents upon my death as follows:

Details and contact information:

....

....

....

9 | Personal Diary

To my loved ones:

○ Yes
I have filled out this section and would like you to review it.

○ No
I have not provided information as this section is not relevant to me.

Details:

Location of diary:

I wish to transfer my personal diary upon my death as follows:

Details and contact information:

10 | Private Letters/Notes

To my loved ones:

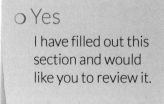

o Yes
I have filled out this section and would like you to review it.

o No
I have not provided information as this section is not relevant to me.

Details:

Location of private letters and notes:

I wish to transfer private letters and notes upon my death as follows:

Details and contact information:

11 | Secrets

To my loved ones:

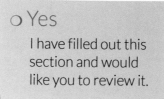

o Yes
I have filled out this section and would like you to review it.

o No
I have not provided information as this section is not relevant to me.

Details:

Location of documents or other paperwork:

I wish to transfer my secrets upon my death as follows:

Details and contact information:

Extra Notes:

"Wisdom is knowing what to do next; virtue is doing it."

–DAVID STARR JORDAN

CHAPTER 6

END-OF-LIFE MATTERS

Empty-handed I entered the world,

Barefoot I leave it.

My coming, my going

Two simple happenings

That got entangled.

-KOZAN ICHIKYO (D. 1360)

Instructions for loved ones to help them with your care as you near the end of your life.

At the end of life, each story is different.

For some people the body weakens while the mind stays alert. Others remain physically strong and cognitive losses take a huge toll. For this reason, it's important to think about and document how you would like to live out your last days before you become too ill to do so.

End-of-life care is the term used to describe the support and medical care given during the time surrounding death.

This chapter may help you communicate your wishes about your care to your loved ones and to caregivers, and prompt an open dialogue about difficult and emotional topics.

In this chapter:

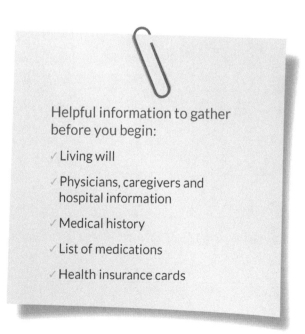

Helpful information to gather before you begin:

✓ Living will

✓ Physicians, caregivers and hospital information

✓ Medical history

✓ List of medications

✓ Health insurance cards

1 Medical and Health Care Directives

Advance directives are important tools for anyone to have because even the healthiest person could experience a sudden accident and not be able to speak for themselves. But when you have a life-threatening illness, it's particularly critical to make clear, in writing, what your wishes are should the time come when you can't express them yourself. There are two ways to do this:

A living will spells out your preferences about certain kinds of life-sustaining treatments. For example, you can indicate whether you do or do not want interventions such as cardiac resuscitation, tube feeding, and mechanical respiration. You may also choose to fill out a DNR/Do Not Resuscitate document. If you have a DNR, please let your loved ones know where this is at all times.

A power of attorney directive names someone that you trust to act as your agent if you are unable to speak for yourself. If you want to choose one person to speak for you on health care matters, and someone else to make financial decisions, you can execute separate financial and health care powers of attorney.

To my loved ones:

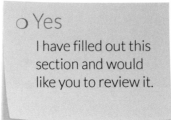

o Yes
I have filled out this section and would like you to review it.

o No
I have not provided information as this section is not relevant to me.

Physician

Contact information:

....

....

Living will

I have a living will: ○ Yes ○ No

Location of living will:

Details:

I have made copies of my living will: ○ Yes ○ No

Location of copies:

Durable power of attorney for health care

I have a durable power attorney for health care: ○ Yes ○ No

Contact information:

Location of documents:

Details:

I have made copies of my durable power of attorney: ○ Yes ○ No

Location of copies:

Do Not Resuscitate document (DNR)

I have a DNR: ○ Yes ○ No

Important! Please make sure that this document is readily at hand and easy to find!

Contact information:

Location of document:

POLST/Physician Orders for Life-Sustaining Treatment

I have a POLST: ○ Yes ○ No

Contact information:

....

....

Location of document:

....

Health insurance card

Details and location of card:

....

Medicare/Medicaid cards

I have Medicare/Medicade cards: ○ Yes ○ No

List of cards:

....

Contact information:

....

....

Location of cards:

....

Medical history

Please list any details from your medical history that you think will be useful for your loved ones. Include relevant contact information and locations for any physicians or medical facilities.

....

....

....

....

....

....

....

Current medications

List and locations of current medications:

_____

_____

_____

_____

_____

_____

_____

_____

Hospital preference

First choice of hospital:

_____

Hospital location:

_____

Contact information:

_____

_____

Second choice of hospital:

_____

Hospital location:

_____

Contact information:

_____

_____

2 | Conversations and Communication

It can be very difficult to talk about death or the process of dying. Your experience will be like no one else's and as you begin getting closer to the end of life, you may have many issues you'd like to discuss and others you'd like to keep private.

This section contains prompts for you to help you think about what you'd like to share with your loved ones or caregivers.

To my loved ones:

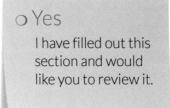

○ Yes
I have filled out this section and would like you to review it.

○ No
I have not provided information as this section is not relevant to me.

I want to talk about my death: ○ Yes ○ No   **I need help to be prepared:** ○ Yes ○ No

I want my end of life experience to be like:

....

....

....

....

....

I worry about the following matters:

....

....

....

....

....

I am most afraid of/uncomfortable about:

I don't wish to be a burden to:

My faith means the following to me in terms of my illness:

I define quality of life as:

What matters most to me is:

....

....

....

....

....

....

I want my family members to respect ALL of my wishes: ○ Yes   ○ No

I want my family to respect my values: ○ Yes   ○ No

I have had conversations with the person I have appointed as my health care proxy: ○ Yes   ○ No

I want to know everything about my medical condition at all times: ○ Yes   ○ No

I want to talk to my family honestly and openly about my health: ○ Yes   ○ No

I want to keep the status of my health private: ○ Yes   ○ No

I want my family to respect my privacy regarding:

....

....

....

....

....

....

I want my friends to respect my privacy regarding:

....

....

....

....

....

I want to know only the basic medical diagnosis and medical information: ○ Yes   ○ No

I want my doctors to guide me and my family in decision-making: ○ Yes   ○ No

I want to be involved in every decision: ○ Yes   ○ No

I want to discuss how long the doctors think I have to live: ○ Yes   ○ No

I want my family and friends to be with me, as much as feasible, until my death: ○ Yes   ○ No

I want to involve a third party person to help family meetings to work through difficult issues: ○ Yes   ○ No

I want to have many conversations with my family about my end of life: ○ Yes   ○ No

I want to have some conversations about my health, but not every day: ○ Yes   ○ No

I want to share my health conditions with those that want to know or ask: ○ Yes   ○ No

I want my family and friends to understand and respect if I change my mind about treatment and choices: ○ Yes   ○ No

I want the following person(s) to communicate with others on my behalf:

....

....

Comments/Notes:

....

....

....

....

....

3 Where Would You Like to be Cared For?

To my loved ones:

○ Yes
I have filled out this section and would like you to review it.

○ No
I have not provided information as this section is not relevant to me.

I would like to be cared for (choose one):

○ At home

○ In a hospital

○ In a nursing facility

I want to only remain close in proximity to my family: ○ Yes ○ No

I am not opposed to treatment in another state or country: ○ Yes ○ No

Comments/Notes:

4 | How Extensive and/or Aggressive Should Your End-of-Life Care Be?

To my loved ones:

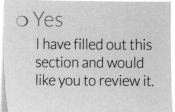

○ Yes
I have filled out this section and would like you to review it.

○ No
I have not provided information as this section is not relevant to me.

I want to have aggressive treatment ○ Yes ○ No

I want to have moderate treatment ○ Yes ○ No

I want to forgo any kind of aggressive treatment ○ Yes ○ No

I want to involve hospice as soon as recommended or needed ○ Yes ○ No

I want to have medications to ease pain but not to fight infection ○ Yes ○ No

Comments/Notes:

....

....

....

....

....

....

....

....

5 | Personal Notes to Family and Friends

To my loved ones:

○ Yes
I have filled out this section and would like you to review it.

○ No
I have not provided information as this section is not relevant to me.

I want my family to know:

....

....

....

....

....

....

I want my friends to know:

....

....

....

....

....

I am most proud of:

I want to mend the following relationships:

I wish I had more time to do:

The most difficult part of dying is:

I want to accomplish the following before I die:

Comments/Notes:

"Words, once they are printed, have a life of their own."

CHAPTER 7

LASTINGMATTERS RESOURCES

WEBSITES

AARP
www.aarp.org

Administration On Aging
www.aoa.gov

Alzheimer's Association
www.alz.org

American Association for Geriatric Psychiatry
www.aagponline.org

American Association of Suicidology
www.suicidology.org

American Cancer Society
www.cancer.org

American Childhood Cancer Organization
www.acco.org

American Heart Association
www.heart.org

American Hospice Foundation
www.americanhospice.org

American Red Cross
www.redcross.org

American Society On Aging
www.asaging.org

American Widow Project
www.americanwidowproject.org

Association For Death Education And Counseling
www.adec.org

Caring Connections
www.caringinfo.org

The Conversation Project
www.theconversationproject.org

Eldercare Locator
www.eldercare.gov

Get Palliative Care
www.getpalliativecare.org

Home Instead Senior Care
www.homeinstead.com

Hospice and Palliative Nurses Association
www.hpna.org

Hospice Foundation Of America
www.hospicefoundation.org

Hospice Net
www.hospicenet.org

In Care Of Dad
www.incareofdad.com

National Alliance for Caregiving
www.caregiving.org

National Cremation Society
www.nationalcremation.com

National Funeral Directors Association
www.nfda.org

National Healthcare Decisions Day
www.nhdd.org

National Military Family Association
www.militaryfamily.org

National Hospice and Palliative Care Organization
www.nhpco.org

The National Kidney Foundation, Inc.
www.kidney.org

Mental Health America
www.mentalhealthamerica.net

National Alliance on Mental Illness
www.nami.org

National Stroke Association
www.stroke.org

Parkinson's Disease Foundation
www.pdf.org

Souring Spirits International
www.sslf.org

Widow's Voice
www.widowsvoice-sslf.blogspot.com

Widow Net
www.widownet.org

BOOKS

On Death and Dying
By Elisabeth Kubler-Ross

Final Gifts
By Maggie Callanan

Dying Well
By Ira Byock, MD

**The Four Things That Matter Most:
A Book About Living**
By Ira Byock, MD

The Last Lecture
By Randy Pausch

The Year of Magical Thinking
By Joan Didion

Living Fully, Dying Well
By Edward W. Bastian and Tina L. Staley

A Grief Observed
By C.S. Lewis

Made in the USA
Coppell, TX
29 October 2020